Contents

Any words appearing in the text in bold, **like this**, are explained in the Glossary.

The watery world

Water covers almost three-quarters of the Earth. Most of it is in the salty oceans – the rest is in freshwater lakes, rivers, streams and marshes. Billions of creatures live in this watery world.

Different habitats

As on land, the waters of the world form many different **habitats**. There are fast-flowing rivers and still lakes, deep, cold ocean waters and shallow, warm **coral reefs**. Different **predators** have **adapted** to life in these varied habitats. Around the coasts and in rivers or lakes, the water is usually fairly shallow and rich in life. Seaweeds, **corals** and water plants provide food and shelter for a huge variety of creatures, all of which can be food for predators. With such a concentration of **prey**, predators don't have to move about much. Some stay in one place and wait for prey to come to them. Others go looking for prey, sneaking up on them or rooting around in places where they hide.

The open ocean

In the open oceans, prey animals are not so easy to find. At one time of year prey might be in one area, then a few months later the good feeding grounds are thousands of kilometres away. Because of this, open ocean predators are great travellers and usually fast swimmers. There is nowhere to hide in the open ocean, so they generally have to chase their prey.

The true top predators in the oceans are humans. We catch billions of tonnes of fish each year, either for sport or food.

Top of the food pyramid

Sharks and some other killer fish in this book are top predators. This means that they are at the end of a chain of connections between sea creatures based on food. The chain starts with tiny, plant-like **microbes** called **algae** (seaweeds are also a kind of algae). Like plants on land, algae use energy from the Sun to make their own food.

Algae provide food for tiny animals, which together with the algae make up the **plankton**. Plankton are food for fish and other larger creatures, and these fish in turn are food for watery predators.

Down in the depths

Conditions deep in the oceans are very different from those at the surface. There is very little light here, and the water is always the same cold temperature. Prey animals are few and far between, so predators must take anything that they can get. Most have huge mouths and stomachs that stretch to swallow prey bigger than themselves.

For detecting prey, deep-sea predators rely on sensing vibrations in the water, or at short range they use long, sensitive feelers. Many deep-sea predators also use some kind of lure to attract prey.

The microscopic creatures that make up plankton. These microbes are diatoms, a kind of algae that have marvellous skeletons made from **silica**.

Piranhas

In a boat on the Orinoco River in Venezuela an angler is fishing. Suddenly his rod starts to jerk – he has caught something! As he reels in the struggling fish, the water around it seems to boil. Hundreds of smaller fish are attacking the angler's catch, biting off chunks of flesh. By the time he gets the fish out of the water, there is little left but bones.

Vicious teeth

There are many stories like this about piranhas. Some **species** have a fearsome reputation, but they are not all so ferocious. Piranhas are quite small fish: the biggest grow to about 60 centimetres long. They have a narrow, flat body, a blunt nose and an upturned jaw rather like a bulldog's. A piranha's mouth is packed with small, razor-sharp, triangular teeth. The teeth in the upper and lower jaws fit neatly together, so that when a piranha bites it completely removes a chunk of flesh.

There are many species of piranha, all of them found only in South American rivers. They differ in size, colour and how they live and feed. White, black-tail and red-bellied piranhas are all fierce **predators**. The golden piranha, however, is not so aggressive. It does eat some meat, but also large amounts of seeds, fruits and other things that fall into the water.

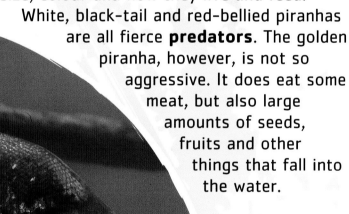

Red-bellied piranhas have the reputation of being the most fearsome piranhas. They have the strongest jaws and the sharpest teeth.

Finding prey

Piranhas prefer to live in 'white-water' rivers, where the water is milky white with **sediment**. To find **prey** in these murky waters, piranhas have an excellent sense of smell. Scientists have found that they can detect a single drop of blood in 200 litres of water!

Piranhas also have excellent hearing – they are very sensitive to vibrations in the water. Vibrations caused by the struggles of an injured or frightened animal in the water can attract several **schools** of piranhas.

When piranhas are hunting, the school spreads out to look for prey. Usually piranhas attack prey animals that are smaller than they are, but sometimes a number of schools will converge on a large animal in a feeding frenzy. In such a frenzy, the piranhas will take a bite out of anything within range – including other piranhas!

If you look inside the mouth of a piranha, you'll understand how they get their fearsome reputation. Its mouth is packed with razor-sharp teeth.

Cow killers

Piranhas have a rather exaggerated reputation as people-killers, but they are certainly cow-killers. Over 1200 cattle a year are killed by piranhas in Brazil.

7

River scavengers

Although piranhas are aggressive **predators**, they aren't fussy eaters. They will eat fish, shellfish, insects, birds, lizards, carrion (dead, rotting meat), fruit, seeds – in fact, almost anything that comes their way. Because piranhas eat just about anything, they play an important part in keeping South American rivers clean. Without piranhas, the rivers would quickly become contaminated with rotting corpses.

Good parents

Piranhas **reproduce** in April or May, just before the tropical rainy season. The female lays thousands of eggs (**spawn**) in the water and the male **fertilizes** them. Most fish leave their eggs to look after themselves, but not piranhas. The eggs are laid in a nest, and the parents protect the nest while the eggs are developing and just after they hatch. The eggs hatch 2 or 3 days after laying. At first the young piranhas eat microscopic creatures, then move on to insects until they are large enough to begin eating meat.

Caimans are one of the piranhas' main predators.

8

A piranha feast

Every year, when the Amazon River is at its lowest, a great wall of water up to 5 metres high roars upstream from the Atlantic Ocean twice each day. This giant wave is called the 'Pororoca'. It is a tidal bore, caused by the tide coming in up the river as a wave, rather than gradually raising the water level. The Pororoca leaves the waters filled with debris, including many animal corpses. It provides a feast for the piranhas, which quickly hoover up the dead and injured.

For most people, the Pororoca is a dangerous nuisance, causing damage to boats and killing animals. However, surfers come to ride the huge waves – although they have to watch out for piranhas if they fall in the water!

Young piranhas are often differently coloured from adults: 'white' piranhas, for instance, are a light, silvery colour when born, but they gradually darken as they get older, and adults are often black.

Piranha enemies

When they are young, piranhas make a tasty mouthful for many river predators. However, even adult piranhas are not safe from predators. Caimans (South American alligators), water snakes, herons and otters all eat piranhas. Humans are also piranha predators – piranhas are good to eat!

European catfish

The catfish floats motionless in the dark water. Only its long whiskers move, feeling for any signs of **prey**. It picks up a vibration – a fish swimming near the surface. Rising up silently from below, it engulfs the fish in its enormous mouth.

Fleshy whiskers

The European catfish, or wels, is a monster, 5 or 6 times bigger than a piranha. European catfish are found in Europe and western Asia. Catfish get their name from their whisker-like feelers, or **barbels**. The European catfish has 6 barbels around its huge, wide mouth. Two of them are very long and mobile. Catfish use barbels to feel around for prey in the darkness. Unlike most fish, catfish have smooth, soft skin with a slimy coating rather than scales.

European catfish like to live in slow-moving water, for instance in marshes, lakes or slow-flowing rivers. In the daytime they rest in a hidden lair, but at night they come out to hunt. European catfish can live for over 100 years and grow to nearly 5 metres. However, no catfish bigger than 3.5 metres have been seen in recent times, because extensive fishing means that the catfish are caught before they can grow to their maximum size.

A European catfish has 6 barbels. The 2 longest, above the mouth, can move around. The 4 on the chin are smaller.

Night hunters

European catfish are night hunters, and find their prey by feel or by sound. They have very good hearing, and can pick up the movements of prey as they swim through the water.

Catfish usually catch small fish that come to the surface at night to feed. However, they will attack almost any animal that is not too large for them to swallow, for instance frogs, ducklings and even sometimes adult swans. Catfish usually glide silently up and grab their prey from below. As well as acting as feelers, some scientists think that the constant movement of the catfish's barbels actually attracts small fish.

Nest-builders

Between May and July, male and female catfish meet up to **spawn**. The male scoops out a shallow nest and the female lays thousands of eggs in it. The male then **fertilizes** the eggs with **sperm**.

Both parents guard the eggs until a few days after they hatch. The **fry** (young fish) that hatch out are about 7 millimetres long and have a **yolk sac** attached to them, which contains food for the first few days after hatching. Once the fry leave the nest, they hide in thick vegetation to avoid **predators**. Even so, many do not make it to adulthood.

European catfish are popular with anglers because they are so big.

Northern pike

A long, slim pike lurks silent and motionless among some reeds. A fish swims towards the reed patch – closer, and closer still. The pike bides its time, waiting for the right moment. Then with a lightning lunge it clamps its jaws tightly round its victim.

Cold-water predator

Like the European catfish the northern pike is a loner, but it hunts by day. This long, muscular fish has an enormous mouth filled with sharp, backward-pointing teeth. Few **prey** ever escape from a pike's jaws.

Northern pike are found across North America, Europe and northern Asia. They live in lakes and slow-moving rivers, usually in shallow water.

Adult pike are dark greeny-brown with lighter vertical bands or blotches on the sides of their bodies. This colouring gives good **camouflage** among the reeds and other plants on the bottom of a river or lake.

Lurking hunters

Because they hunt by day, pike have excellent eyesight. Their eyes face forwards, which gives them good **binocular vision** and helps them to judge distances accurately.

Pike are usually 'lie-in-wait' **predators**, catching unwary fish from a hiding place. Pike also sometimes stalk their victims, swimming menacingly closer before a quick attack.

A large pike catching a trout. Trout are also predatory fish, and sometimes a large trout will catch and eat a small pike!

12

Adult pike mostly eat other fish, especially trout. However, they will attack almost anything that will fit into their mouth – including other pike! Sometimes they catch fish that are too long to swallow. If this happens, the pike swims around with the victim's tail sticking out of its mouth until the head has been **digested**.

Early breeders

Pike **spawn** from about February onwards, which is earlier than other fish in the same **habitat**. The females release thousands of eggs in shallow water, and the males **fertilize** them with their **sperm**.

The young pike hatch after about 15 days. At hatching they still have a **yolk sac**, and they attach themselves to plants and feed on the yolk for 6 days or so.

By the time the eggs of other fish hatch out, the young pike are several weeks old. They are big enough to be able to catch and eat the other **hatchlings**.

A pike has to survive many hazards before it is fully grown. Newly hatched pikes are only a few millimetres long and are easy prey for many fish. As they grow, pike become prey for larger predators such as **ospreys**. However, their main enemies are other pike.

Because they are born earlier in the year, pike young are bigger than the young of prey **species**. They are often 15 centimetres long by the end of their first summer.

13

Archer fish

An insect sits sunning itself above a mangrove swamp in Australia. One moment it is there, then – plop! The insect is struggling in the water. An archer fish has scored another direct hit.

Flattened and stripy

There are several kinds of archer fish, most of which live in Australia and South-east Asia. They are small fish, up to 30 centimetres long. The front part of the archer fish's body is narrow and flat, which makes it difficult to see from above. It has a pattern of black stripes or blotches on its body, which give excellent **camouflage** in sun-dappled water.

Archer fish live in river **estuaries** and **mangrove** swamps, and they feed mainly on insects and spiders. The archer fish is a daytime hunter, and relies on good eyesight. Its eyes are set forward on the head, which gives it a good ability to judge distances.

Straight shooter

Archer fish hunt near the water surface, looking for insects perched on plants nearby. Often they leap up out of the water and grab an insect perched on a twig or leaf. They can leap their own height out of water.

If an insect is too far away to grab, the archer fish will try to shoot it down. It can shoot a jet of water out of its mouth a distance of up to 3 metres.

If **prey** is close enough, archer fish prefer to jump up for it rather than shooting.

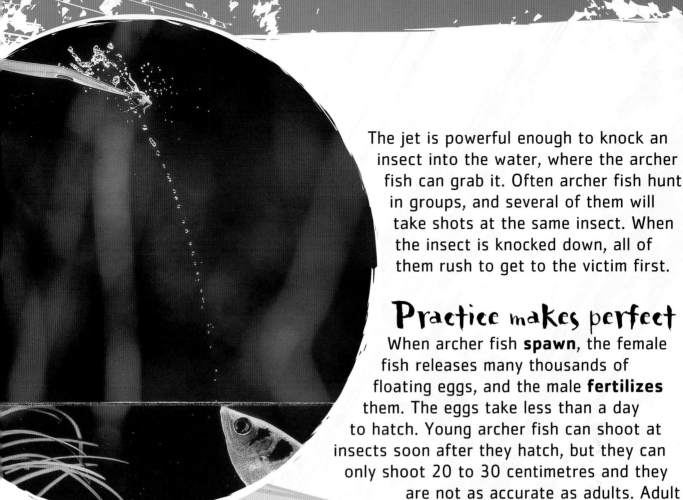

The jet is powerful enough to knock an insect into the water, where the archer fish can grab it. Often archer fish hunt in groups, and several of them will take shots at the same insect. When the insect is knocked down, all of them rush to get to the victim first.

Practice makes perfect

When archer fish **spawn**, the female fish releases many thousands of floating eggs, and the male **fertilizes** them. The eggs take less than a day to hatch. Young archer fish can shoot at insects soon after they hatch, but they can only shoot 20 to 30 centimetres and they are not as accurate as adults. Adult archer fish hit their target 99 times out of 100!

An archer fish has a groove in the roof of its mouth, which forms a tube when the fish presses its tongue against it. It shoots water through this tube by snapping shut its **gills**.

Correcting the bend

If you put one end of something straight in a glass of water, it seems to bend where it goes into the water. This is because light bends (refracts) as it travels from air into water or from water into air. Archer fish fire from below the water surface. This means they have to correct for this bending when they shoot at an insect.

Tiger shark

uring the day, the tiger shark rests in deep water many kilometres from the **coral reef**, but at night it comes close to shore to hunt. Cruising through the reef waters, its sharp senses of smell and hearing are always on the alert for food. With its huge, powerful jaws and awesome saw teeth, it is more than a match for any creature there.

Built for hunting

Sharks and their relatives are different from most other fish because their skeleton is not made of bone but of a lighter, more flexible material called **cartilage**. This means that sharks are light and agile for their size. Sharks are **predators**, and they are well designed for the job of hunting. Sharks have sharp senses to help them find their **prey**. Their muscular, **streamlined** bodies help them to move in fast once they find a victim. And their strong jaws and sharp, pointed teeth make sure that prey cannot get away once they are caught.

Eating machine

Tiger sharks grow up to 6 metres long. They get their name from the dark stripes that young sharks have on their back. A tiger shark has notched and saw-edged teeth that allow it to eat all kinds of tough food. They will eat almost anything. Sharks have been found with beer bottles, coal and even car number plates in their stomachs.

Because they are not fussy eaters, they can be dangerous to humans: many shark attacks are due to tiger sharks.

A tiger shark's fearsome teeth allow it to crunch through bones, the shells of sea turtles and the tough skin of other sharks.

The jaws of this tiger shark are made of springy cartilage rather than bone, but its fearsome saw-edged teeth are very hard and sharp.

Sharp senses

Tiger sharks hunt at night, and their most important sense for finding prey is smell. A tiger shark's nose can pick up blood and animal smells from many kilometres away. As the shark moves, water flows through its nostrils and over folds of skin covered with highly sensitive cells that pick up 'smell chemicals' in the water. Sharks also have very good hearing. They can hear sounds much lower in pitch than humans.

Hunters from birth

Instead of releasing their eggs into the water (**spawning**) like most fish, sharks **mate**. This means that the male shark's **sperm fertilizes** the female's eggs while the eggs are still in her body. In most sharks the eggs develop inside the female's body, and she gives birth to live **pups** (baby sharks).

Female tiger sharks give birth to as many as 80 pups in one **brood**. The pups have a full set of teeth and are ready to hunt as soon as they are born.

This is a magnified view of a shark's tough, protective skin. The skin is made of lots of tiny tooth-like scales called denticles. As well as protecting the shark, denticles help it to swim faster.

17

Whitetip reef shark

The diver is exploring the tropical reef, shining his torch into cracks and crevices in the **coral**. He comes across a bigger hole: a cave that looks large enough to swim into. But when he gets closer, he sees that the cave is occupied. A group of whitetip reef sharks are resting there, stacked in the cave like a pile of logs.

Night senses

Whitetip reef sharks are common in the warm, shallow waters of tropical reefs. These small, slim sharks are often found resting in caves or on the sea bed during the day. But at night they wake up and go hunting.

Like the tiger shark, whitetips hunt using their sharp hearing and excellent sense of smell. They also use their lateral line **organs** to help them get around at night. Along each side, sharks (and other fish) have 2 long, water-filled tubes, called lateral lines. The insides of the lateral line organs contain sensitive hairs that detect **pressure** changes in the water.

The lateral line acts as a depth detector (water pressure increases with depth), but it can also detect waves in the water made by the swimming movements of fish.

The shark itself also makes pressure waves as it swims. As it approaches an object such as a rock, the shark's own pressure wave changes. The lateral line organs sense these changes, so the shark can avoid obstacles in the dark.

Whitetip reef sharks are about 1 to 2 metres long. They get their name from the small white patches on the tip of the large dorsal (back) fin and on the tail.

18

Hunting methods

Coral reefs have many cracks and gaps where fish and other sea creatures can hide from **predators**. These nooks and crannies are the whitetips' hunting grounds. They swim over the reef, investigating likely hiding places and winkling out **prey**. If an opening is too small for the shark to get into, it will break the surrounding coral to make a bigger gap.

Live young

Like tiger sharks, whitetip reef sharks give birth to live young. Once the eggs have been **fertilized**, they take at least 5 months to develop. The **pups** are nourished by a **yolk sac** as they grow inside the mother shark.

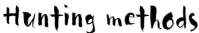

Ocean cousin

Although they have white tips to their **fins**, oceanic whitetip sharks like the one above are very different from their reef-living cousins. They are much bigger and have very large fins. They are also much more aggressive and dangerous. Most sharks circle their prey before attacking, but oceanic whitetips don't waste time: they go straight into the attack.

Barracuda

The great barracuda moves lazily through the waters of the tropical reef. At times it hangs motionless, barely moving its **fins**. But then it sees a **school** of small fish that have come a little too close for safety. With a tremendous burst of speed the barracuda is among them, spearing **prey** on its razor-sharp teeth.

Buoyed up with air

Great barracudas generally live in warm waters around **coral reefs**. Adult fish can be up to 2 metres long, and live for about 14 years. Unlike sharks, barracudas have a skeleton made of bone rather than **cartilage**. This means that they are heavier than sharks of the same size. To make themselves more **buoyant**, bony fish have a **swim bladder** that they can fill with air. A bony fish can gulp in air to fill its swim bladder to make itself more buoyant, or let out air if it wants to swim deeper.

Top predators

Great barracudas are daytime hunters, and they use eyesight to spot their prey. On the tropical reefs where they live they are the top **predators**. Only humans and the occasional large shark pose any threat to an adult great barracuda.

A great barracuda has two sets of teeth. The outer teeth are smaller and razor sharp, while the inner teeth are larger and like daggers.

Slash attack

Barracudas usually catch their prey with a sudden headlong rush. They can accelerate from zero to almost 60 km/h (35 mph) in a few seconds. A barracuda's narrow body is difficult to see from head-on – the angle that its prey sees it from – and in open water its silvery sides make it even harder to spot. Young barracudas can change colour to match the surrounding vegetation, and dark bars appear on their sides. This barring breaks up the barracuda's shape while it hides among plants.

Barracudas feed on a wide variety of fish and other prey. They can open their mouths very wide to eat many fish whole, and they deal with larger prey by chopping them in half with their razor-sharp teeth.

From egg to adult

Barracudas are thought to **spawn** in open water, but there has been little research into the subject. Females can lay up to 300,000 eggs each year. The eggs hatch into small **larvae**, which are carried by the ocean currents. Once the young reach a length of about 5 centimetres they move to sheltered areas of seagrass or **mangroves**, where they stay until they are over a year old. Male barracudas take about 2 years to become adults, while females are not mature until they are 4 years old.

Great barracudas usually hunt alone. However their smaller relatives, chevron barracuda, live and hunt together in large schools.

Red lionfish

The red lionfish is only about the length of the diver's forearm, but its long, spiny fins make it look bigger. When it sees the diver the lionfish doesn't swim away – it advances, fins pointing forward. The diver decides to give the fish a wide berth. The long spines that support its fins are tipped with a poisonous venom that can kill its **prey** – or give humans a very painful sting.

Lie-in-wait predator

The red lionfish is found around the coasts of Australia, South-east Asia and Japan. In the daytime a lionfish's striking colours and markings are a warning to **predators** that the lionfish would not make a good snack. However, at dawn and at dusk, when the light fades, the lionfish's colours fade, and the stripes along its body break up its outline. The long fins look like harmless **filter feeders** called feather stars. If the lionfish hangs motionless in the water, its fins waving gently, fish will sooner or later come swimming by. When one comes close enough, the lionfish sucks in water through its mouth – and with it the prey. The whole process takes just a split second.

Sometimes lionfish hunt in small groups or packs. They corner their prey against rocks, spreading their huge fins to cut off any escape.

Lionfish are not afraid of people: if a diver comes across a lionfish it will usually stand its ground with fins spread wide.

Balls of eggs

Lionfish **spawn** in groups, with the males **fertilizing** the females' eggs as soon as they are released. The eggs are covered in a jelly-like coating, which swells in the water to form a ball.

The lionfish eggs take 1 to 2 days to hatch. When the young first emerge they are only about one millimetre long, but they grow quickly, doubling in size in the first day or so.

Fish can mistake the fins of a lionfish for a harmless feather star like this one.

Other stingers

Lionfish belong to a **family** of poisonous fish known as scorpion fish. Another member of the family, the stonefish, is probably the most poisonous fish in the sea. The stonefish is amazingly well **camouflaged** to look like a large pebble or a stone. The spines on its back contain an immensely strong poison that can kill a person.

The porcupine fish, below, is poisonous, but it also has another way of deterring predators. Its body is covered in short spines, which normally lie flat. But if the fish is attacked it puffs up into a spiny ball, making itself a very unpleasant mouthful!

23

Dogfish

The fishermen have made a good catch, and are hauling in a net bulging with mackerel. But as they haul the net in, hundreds of spiny dogfish appear. They bite through the net and attack the mackerel inside. The fishermen's catch is either eaten by the dogfish or escapes through the holes the dogfish make in the net.

Spiny dogfish

Spiny dogfish are small cold-water sharks, about 90 to 120 centimetres long. They have a small spine in front of each of their two dorsal (back) **fins**. During the winter they spend their time deep in the ocean, but in summer they **migrate** to shallower waters.

Spiny dogfish are the most abundant of all sharks. Their main **prey** animals are fish such as mackerel and herring, but they also catch squid, crabs, shrimps and jellyfish. Dogfish often hunt in groups of hundreds or even thousands of fish. Like most other sharks, spiny dogfish **mate** and give birth to live **pups**. The pups are not born until 18 months or 2 years after mating: this is probably the longest **gestation period** of any shark. Young males take about 11 years to mature, while females take up to 19 years. Spiny dogfish also live a long time – they have been known to reach 70 years of age.

The spines of the spiny dogfish are mildly poisonous to humans.

Although schools of spiny dogfish often attack fishermen's nets and steal the fish, sometimes the dogfish themselves get caught in the nets.

Green dogfish

Green dogfish are much smaller than spiny dogfish. They grow to a maximum of about 25 centimetres long. They live in the warm waters of the Gulf of Mexico, spending most of their time deep below the surface. Scientists think that these fierce **predators** hunt in groups. All green dogfish that have been caught by fishermen have had only the remains of squid and octopuses in their stomachs. These are creatures much bigger than the dogfish themselves, which they would be unable to catch alone. Green dogfish have patterns of lights along their sides, which may help them to stay together in the darkness of the deep ocean.

Cookie-cutter sharks

The cookie-cutter is another fairly small shark that is related to the green and spiny dogfishes. Cookie-cutter sharks have light organs on their belly that act as **camouflage**: any fish seeing the cookie-cutter from below sees a light glow that blends in with the light from the surface.

Cookie-cutter sharks feed on creatures far bigger than themselves, such as dolphins and tuna. However, a cookie-cutter doesn't kill its victims: it simply takes a bite out of them. Its fearsome teeth cut a neat oval plug from the victim's flesh, like a cookie-cutter making a biscuit-shaped hole in cookie dough (see photo).

Gulpers, lancetfish and anglerfish

Inside the small submarine it is warm and light. But outside, over a thousand metres below the ocean surface, the water is pitch black and freezing cold. If either of the two scientists in the sub were to swim outside, the tremendous **pressure** of the water would crush them. But through the window of the submarine they can see strange creatures that can survive at these depths – including deep-sea **predators** such as gulper eels, anglerfish and lancetfish.

Gulper eels

The ocean depths support far fewer creatures than the surface waters. This makes it much harder for deep-water predators to find **prey**.

Gulper eels are about 60 centimetres long, with a large head, huge jaws and a thin, soft body. They have **adapted** in many ways to survive on a scarce food supply. For a start, a gulper eel saves energy by staying in one place and waiting for prey, rather than chasing around in the dark. Because it doesn't swim much, the gulper doesn't need many muscles. When prey does come along, it's important that the gulper eel can eat it. This is where its huge mouth comes in. Gulpers aren't fussy eaters: they will grab just about anything. And having such an enormous mouth means that the gulper can eat creatures much bigger than the eel itself.

Gulper eels are so well adapted to the depths that they cannot survive in the low pressures of surface waters. This explains why no live gulper eels have ever been caught.

Lancetfish

Lancetfish are among the largest deep-sea predators, growing to over 2 metres in length. They often come up closer to the surface, where they can find more food. Lancetfish have a snake-like body, a large mouth, and a high, sail-like **fin** on their back. Creatures as big as yellowfin tuna, squid, octopus and shrimps are among the many animals that lancetfish catch and eat. Gulper eels and other deep-sea fish are also sometimes on their menu.

Little is known about how lancetfish grow and **reproduce**. Each fish has both male and female **sex organs** when it is young, then it becomes either male or female when it matures.

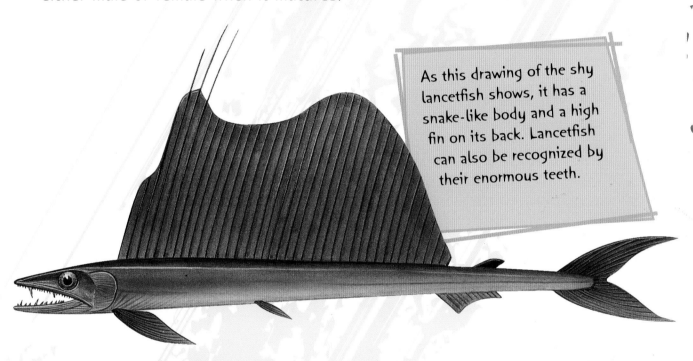

As this drawing of the shy lancetfish shows, it has a snake-like body and a high fin on its back. Lancetfish can also be recognized by their enormous teeth.

Marathon journeys

Some deep-sea fish make long journeys every day – to the surface of the sea and back down again. These predators move up to the surface at night to catch prey, then go back to the depths in the day for safety. The journey can be over 2000 metres there and back. Since some of the fish are only 25 centimetres long or less, this is equivalent to a human running 2 marathons a day!

Anglerfish

The fish that probably live deeper than any others are deep-sea anglerfish. There are over 250 types of anglerfish, about 150 of which live in the deep sea. Most are small (less than 10 centimetres long), but a few **species** can reach 50 centimetres in length.

In an anglerfish, part of the dorsal (back) fin forms a kind of 'fishing line' on the top of its head with a 'lure' on the end of it. The lure is **luminous** – it shines out in the darkness and attracts other deep-sea fish. The anglerfish can make the lure flash, to make it even more enticing.

Once a victim comes close enough, the anglerfish grabs it in its huge jaws. An anglerfish's mouth is not quite as big as that of a gulper eel, but it can still swallow prey bigger than itself.

Stick-on males

Female anglerfish are active predators, but the males do not eat at all. Their one aim in life is to find a female.

When a male anglerfish does find a female, he attaches himself to her body. Once attached, the male gradually fuses (joins) with the female. The only parts of the male that remain active are his sex organs. This means that whenever the female releases her eggs, the male's **sperm** is ready to **fertilize** them.

Anglerfish like this one have been found at depths of over 8000 metres. The luminous lure will attract any prey in these dark conditions.

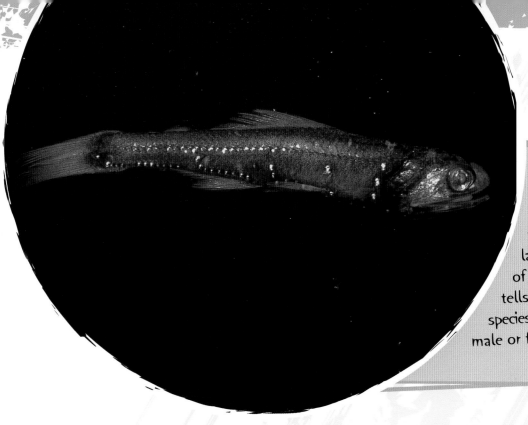

The various kinds of lanternfish are the most common fish in deeper waters. A lanternfish has a pattern of lights on its body that tells other lanternfish what species it is and whether it is male or female.

Lights in the deep

Nine out of ten deep-sea fish produce light through special chemical reactions. This light-producing ability is known as bioluminescence.

Deep-sea fish use lights in many different ways. Some kinds, like the anglerfish, use light to attract prey. Others, such as the various kinds of lanternfish, have patterns of lights that probably help them to identify each other in the dark.

What little light makes it to the ocean depths is blue. Red light does not penetrate this deep. Many creatures are coloured red, which makes them invisible in the faint blue light. But one fish, the stoplight loosejaw, can see through this red disguise. The loosejaw has two red 'searchlights' on its head. In these lights, the red shrimps that the loosejaw hunts show up brightly.

Thresher shark

"Whoa, look over there!" calls the captain. The passengers on the nature cruise rush to the side of the boat as a thresher shark leaps from the water taking it completely clear of the sea. One passenger has his camera, but the shark is back in the water before he can snap it.

Ocean travellers

Thresher sharks are agile sharks with a very long tail. They can be up to 6 metres long, but half this length is tail. Threshers are travelling, open-ocean sharks, but they also sometimes spend time closer to shore. In spring, for instance, thresher sharks in the Pacific Ocean are often seen off the coast of California, USA and in summer Atlantic thresher sharks are common close to the Isle of Wight in southern Britain.

Hunting methods

Thresher sharks eat squid, octopuses and fish that swim in large groups, such as mackerel, herring and anchovies. They are thought to use their long tails to herd groups of fish into a tight bunch. The sharks may also slap their tails on the water surface, to frighten the fish into groups.

Once the fish are bunched together, threshers charge through the group, snapping left and right as they go. Many fish are stunned or injured, and the threshers can then eat them at leisure.

Threshers are very athletic sharks. If they miss prey near the surface, they will sometimes jump completely out of the water to try to catch it.

Warm-blooded sharks

Most sharks and other fish are 'cold-blooded'. This means that they do not have a way of keeping their body temperature higher than that of their surroundings.

Threshers, however, are part of a group called the mackerel sharks that can raise their body temperature above that of their surroundings when they are in cold water. Heat generated by the sharks as they swim is used to keep their muscles warm. Keeping the muscles warm in this way means that that these sharks can keep active and move fast, even in cold waters. This is a great advantage to a **predator** that needs to chase its **prey**.

Egg-eating young

As with most other sharks, threshers' eggs are **fertilized** inside the female's body. The male shark has extensions of the **pelvic fins** called 'claspers' that are used to transfer **sperm** to the female. Once the sperm fertilize the eggs, they grow and hatch inside the mother. The mother produces more, unfertilized eggs, and the growing young feed on these eggs inside her. At birth the shark **pups** are 1 to 1.5 metres long. At about 9 months old, they are ready to hunt.

The thresher has small jaws for a shark. Its usual prey are smallish fish that swim in shoals, like these young chevron barracuda.

Great white shark

The great white shark cruises 20 metres below the surface, all its senses alert for **prey**. It 'hears' the elephant seal first, feeling the vibrations of the seal swimming (sounds are made by vibrations in the water). Moving in closer, the shark sees the elephant seal's silhouette above. It attacks from below with terrible speed and power, disabling the large seal with one tremendous bite.

Tremendous teeth

The great white lives in coastal waters around the world, but it also travels widely. It prefers cooler waters, but is occasionally seen in tropical seas.

Great whites can grow to almost 6.5 metres long and weigh over 3 tonnes. Their jaws are tremendously powerful, and contain up to 3000 teeth. The first two rows of teeth are used for biting prey. Behind these are rows of growing teeth ready to move into place when a tooth is damaged or lost.

The great white lives mostly in coastal waters, but it also travels across the oceans. Like thresher sharks, great whites can keep their muscles warm while swimming, so they can hunt in cooler waters.

A great white's teeth can be up to 7.5 cm long. But they don't compare with this tooth of the prehistoric shark *Megalodon*. From its teeth, scientists estimate that *Megalodon* may have measured 12 metres long, or more.

All kinds of food

Great white sharks are adaptable hunters: they catch whatever prey is abundant in a particular area. They hunt large and small fish, other sharks, seals (including huge elephant seals), sea lions and dolphins. They are sometimes scavengers, eating dead whales and fish. And occasionally they will also attack people.

Great whites rarely eat sea birds or sea otters. Off the coast of South Africa, for instance, penguins have often been found killed by an 'exploratory' bite from a great white, where the shark has 'tasted' the penguin then decided it is not good to eat. Great whites also come up under seabirds or sea otters sitting on the water and toss them into the air, but do not eat them.

Making a Kill

Like other sharks, great whites use their excellent senses of smell and hearing to detect prey at a distance. Other sharks often circle their prey before they attack, but great whites usually make a direct approach. They come from below and behind, and the victim does not see the shark approaching. With smaller prey, such as young sea lions, the shark swallows its victim in one tremendous mouthful. When catching seals and sea lions, the shark may come right out of the water as it grabs its victim!

Despite their size, great whites are incredibly athletic. They can jump clear out of the water when catching prey at the surface.

People Killers?

Great whites are the sharks that people most fear, and with good reason. Great whites are responsible for more shark attacks on humans than any other kind of shark. But, in fact, great whites rarely attack humans, even though they often hunt close to beaches where people swim.

When a great white does attack, it usually does so for one of two reasons. The shark might see a human as a threat to its territory, and attack to drive them away. The shark might give only a 'warning bite', but it can still cause serious injury.

The other reason great whites might attack is if they are hungry and mistake a person for food. Someone on a surfboard can look like a seal when seen from below.

People do not have enough blubber (fat) on them to make a good meal for a great white. In most cases the shark will bite once and then realize its mistake. However, if an attack causes an injury producing lots of blood, this can stimulate the shark to attack again.

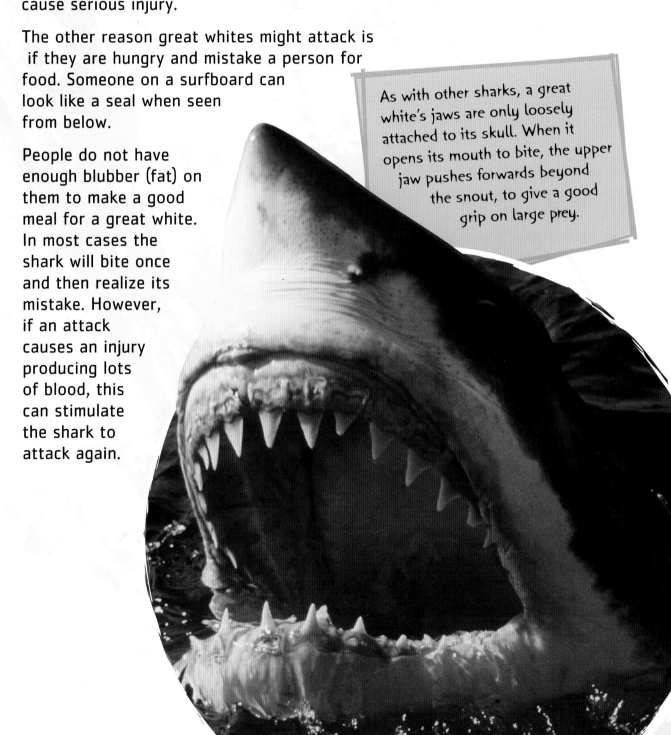

As with other sharks, a great white's jaws are only loosely attached to its skull. When it opens its mouth to bite, the upper jaw pushes forwards beyond the snout, to give a good grip on large prey.

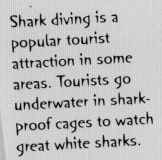

Shark diving is a popular tourist attraction in some areas. Tourists go underwater in shark-proof cages to watch great white sharks.

Sharks in danger

Great whites can be a danger to people, but people are much more of a danger to great whites. In most areas around the world, the numbers of great whites are falling. There are several threats to great white sharks. They are not fished for food, but large numbers are killed because their jaws and teeth can be sold for high prices, and sport fishermen like to catch great whites because they are impressive fish.

Another reason for great white deaths is accidental capture. When they scavenge fish or other creatures caught in nets or on fishing lines, great whites sometimes get hooked or entangled, and often die before they can be released. Because of the different threats to great whites, they are now protected **species** in many areas where they are found.

Biggest fish of all

The great white is the biggest predatory fish in the world, but it is a tiddler compared to its relative the whale shark. The whale shark is the largest fish in the sea. There are reports of individuals up to 18 metres long! Its enormous mouth is lined with thousands of teeth – but they are all very tiny. Whale sharks are harmless **filter feeders**, that vacuum up huge quantities of microscopic **plankton**, and sometimes small fish. Another filter feeder, the basking shark, is also much bigger than the great white. It can grow to over 12 metres in length.

Hammerhead shark

A great hammerhead shark is chasing a stingray. The stingray swims close to the seabed, twisting and turning to try to escape, but the hammerhead is too fast. Swimming above the ray, it swings its head down and pins the ray to the seabed. Then, pivoting on its nose, the hammerhead takes a huge bite out of one of the stingray's **fins**.

A hammer-shaped head

There are several kinds of hammerhead shark, ranging from the small bonnethead sharks, which can be up to about 1.5 metres long, to the great hammerheads, which can measure over 4 metres. Smaller hammerheads eat small fish and squid, while larger **species** attack bigger **prey**, including other sharks.

The hammerhead's wide, flattened head looks rather like a wing, and this is no accident. It is in fact a 'water wing', which gives extra lift as the hammerhead moves forwards and it makes swimming more efficient. It also makes it easier for the shark to twist and turn, which is helpful when chasing prey.

Super senses

A hammerhead shark's wide head also allows more room for sense **organs**. Hammerheads have good eyesight and, like other sharks, they have an excellent sense of smell and good hearing.

At close range, sharks use a sixth sense that we don't have. They are sensitive to weak electrical currents in the water, which fish and other creatures produce when they move. Hammerheads have been shown to have a better electrical sense than other sharks.

The wing-like head of a hammerhead helps in swimming, makes fast turns easier and improves the shark's senses.

The whip-like tail of a stingray has a needle-sharp sting. The largest stingrays have a jagged sting as large as a bread knife.

Poisonous prey

The favourite prey of great hammerhead sharks are stingrays. Stingrays have a painful sting in their tail, but hammerheads do not seem to be bothered by this. One hammerhead was found to have 96 stingray barbs in its head! Other poisonous fish are also on the hammerhead's menu. Pufferfish and trunkfish both produce deadly poisons, but hammerheads seem to be able to eat them without any ill effects.

Social sharks

Great hammerhead sharks live alone, but scalloped hammerheads get together in large groups. At night the scalloped hammerheads hunt alone, then gather together each day. Gathering in large numbers protects the sharks from **predators** such as larger sharks and killer whales. The gatherings are also connected with **mating**. Females form a circle, with the older, stronger ones at the centre. The males then battle to get into the centre of the group and mate with the strongest females.

Like other sharks, hammerheads give birth to live **pups**. However, the pups are nourished directly from their mother, not by a **yolk sac** or by eating eggs that were not **fertilized**.

Hundreds of scalloped hammerheads, like this one, gather at seamounts (submarine mountains) in the middle of the ocean. They are thought to use the seamounts as navigational marks – to help them find their way around.

Marlin, sailfish and swordfish

A group of sailfish has found a shoal of mackerel. Swimming around and below them, the sailfish herd the mackerel into a tight bunch close to the surface, where they cannot easily escape. The sailfish then take it in turns to attack the tightly packed fish, while the rest of the group stops victims escaping.

Ocean racers

Sailfish, marlin and swordfish are all known as billfish because they have long, spear-like snouts or bills. If sharks are tigers of the ocean, then billfish are the cheetahs. These ocean racers are built for speed. The speediest are sailfish, which can swim at 110 km/h (68 mph) for short periods.

Marlin

There are several kinds of marlin. All of them are large, but blue marlin are the biggest. They grow to a length of nearly 4.5 metres and can weigh 900 kilograms. Female marlin are bigger than the males.

Like other billfish, marlin are very athletic and can make huge leaps out of the water. They may do this to get rid of **parasitic** fish that attach themselves to the marlin's body.

Apart from its size, the dorsal (back) **fin** is the main difference between a marlin and a sailfish. A marlin's dorsal fin makes a high point at the front then slopes away at the back. To make itself more **streamlined** when swimming fast, the marlin can fold away its pectoral (side) fins into grooves on its sides.

Marlin are powerful, aggressive hunters. Their usual **prey** are fish that swim in **schools**, such as herring, mackerel, hake and dorado. They also hunt squid. They usually hunt in the upper part of the ocean, where the water is warmest.

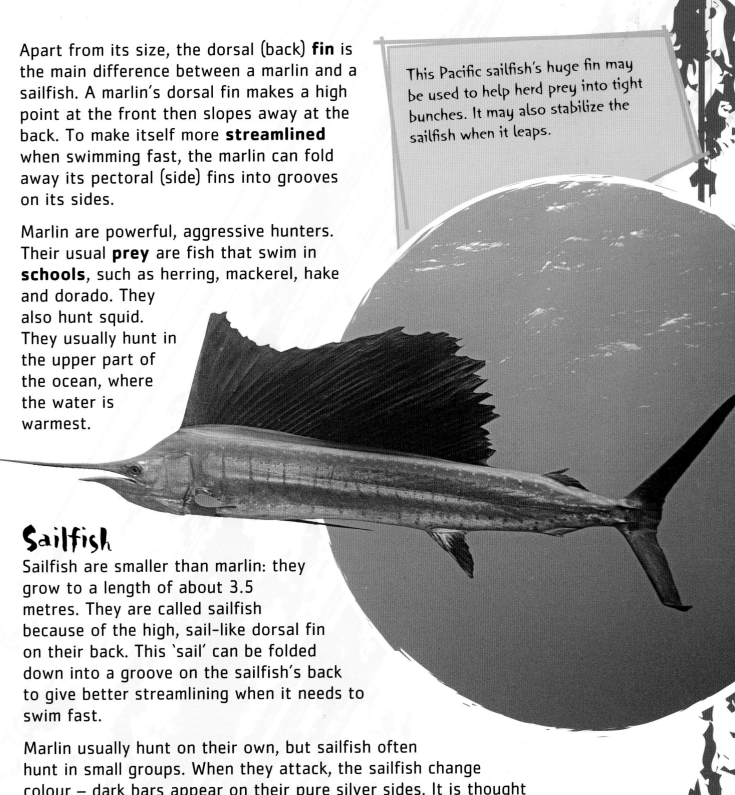

This Pacific sailfish's huge fin may be used to help herd prey into tight bunches. It may also stabilize the sailfish when it leaps.

Sailfish

Sailfish are smaller than marlin: they grow to a length of about 3.5 metres. They are called sailfish because of the high, sail-like dorsal fin on their back. This 'sail' can be folded down into a groove on the sailfish's back to give better streamlining when it needs to swim fast.

Marlin usually hunt on their own, but sailfish often hunt in small groups. When they attack, the sailfish change colour – dark bars appear on their pure silver sides. It is thought the stripes may confuse the sailfish's prey.

Like other billfish, sailfish **spawn** in the open ocean. The female releases huge numbers of eggs – 4 or 5 million per female – that are then **fertilized** by the males. The eggs float with the ocean currents until they hatch. The young sailfish grow very fast – by the end of their first year they can be 1.5 metres long.

Swordfish

Swordfish are different in several ways from other billfish. Their bodies are smooth and scaleless, and they have no teeth. Also, a swordfish's bill is flat, with sharp edges, whereas other billfish have round, pointed bills.

Swordfish hunt at night rather than during the day. In the daytime they sun themselves by cruising slowly along near the water surface. They hunt all kinds of fish, including deep-water kinds such as silver hake and lanternfish.

All billfish are thought to use their bill for feeding, but swordfish definitely use their bill as a weapon. When they attack a **school** of fish they charge into them, slashing from side to side with their sharp bill. This injures or stuns many fish, and the swordfish can then turn back and eat them at leisure.

Millions of eggs

Swordfish produce even more eggs than other billfish. A large female can lay up to 30 million eggs, with each one about a millimetre across. The **fry** have a silvery, snake-like body and the bill is not yet developed. They grow more slowly than sailfish, and take 4 years or more to mature. Females grow faster and live longer than male swordfish.

Swordfish are found in warm oceans around the world. They can grow to over 4 metres, but about one third of this length is the bill.

Billfish are large, strong, athletic fish that sea anglers like to try and catch. Sometimes the anglers will kill them, but nowadays they more often return them to the sea.

Billfish in danger

Since the 1960s, the numbers of billfish in the oceans have fallen rapidly. The main cause for this has been new methods of fishing, especially longlining. Longlining is fishing with lines up to 40 kilometres long, each with hundreds or thousands of hooks on it. It is a good way to catch large fish such as tuna and swordfish. However, too many fish are being caught, and their numbers are falling. The average size of the fish is falling too, which means that the fish being caught are getting younger. This is worrying because it is important for the fish to become adults and **reproduce** before they are caught.

Bluefin tuna

It is 5 a.m. at the fish market in Tokyo, and a single bluefin tuna is up for sale. The bidding is fast and furious, and the smaller bidders quickly drop out as the price climbs. At last the auctioneer bangs his hammer: 'Sold – for 10 million yen!' (£50,000).

Biggest tuna

Bluefin tuna are the biggest **species** of tuna, and the most valuable fish in the world. Adult bluefins can grow to 4.5 metres long and weigh up to 800 kilograms. Small tuna are **prey** to many different **predators**, but bluefin tuna have only the biggest sharks, killer whales and humans to fear.

Cooler waters

Bluefin tuna live in cooler waters than billfish. They can thrive in cooler areas because tuna fish, like thresher and great white sharks, can transfer heat from their muscles into their blood.

Bluefins are always on the move. Like most sharks and many other fish, tuna must keep swimming or they will die. Tuna swim with their mouths open, which pushes water over their **gills**. If they stop swimming there is no water flowing over the gills, and they cannot get oxygen from the water.

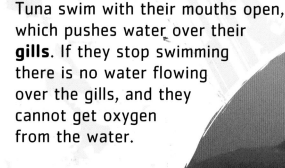

Bluefins are designed to travel fast for long distances. Their wide tail provides the power, and their bodies are highly **streamlined** so that they slip easily through the water.

Squadron hunters

Like other tuna, bluefins swim together in **schools** or squadrons. Each squadron is made up of fish that are about the same size. When they are looking for prey, the squadron spreads out in a long line. Once they have found prey, bluefins attack at great speed. Their main prey are schooling fish such as anchovies and mackerel. These prey are much smaller than the bluefins, which swallow them in a gulp.

Millions of eggs

Tuna fish produce millions of eggs when they **spawn**: a large female bluefin can produce 10 million eggs in a year. However, very few eggs survive to become adult fish. In their first year the young tuna grow to about 60 centimetres long, but they take between 4 and 8 years to become fully mature. This is much slower than other tuna, which are fully grown within 1 or 2 years.

Fished to the limits

Because they are so valuable, fishing fleets hunt down bluefin tuna wherever they can find them. Many bluefins have been killed, and large, fully grown bluefins are now extremely rare. If overfishing continues, they will die out altogether. This photo shows tuna being unloaded from a Japanese longline fishing ship on to a factory ship.

Classification charts

By comparing the characteristics of different living things, scientists can classify them (sort them into groups). A **species** is a group of animals or plants that are closely related. Similar species are put together in a larger group called a genus (plural genera). Similar genera are grouped into **families**, and so on through classes, orders and phyla to the largest groups – kingdoms. Fish are part of the animal kingdom. They are divided into two classes, the bony fish (Osteichthyes) and the **cartilaginous** fish (Chondrichthyes).

Bony fish

Over 95 per cent of all fish are bony fish. The main orders are shown below.

Order	Number of Families	Number of Species	Examples
Anguilliformes	15	over 700	eels
Saccopharyngiformes	4	29	swallowers, gulper eels
Cypriniformes	6	3500	carp, suckers, loaches
Characiformes	12	over 1300	piranhas, tetras, darters
Siluriformes	34	2500	catfish
Esociformes	2	10	pike
Osmeriformes	13	307	smelt, noodlefish
Salmoniformes	1	over 150	salmon
Aulopiformes	13	219	telescope fish, lancetfish
Myctophiformes	2	241	lanternfish
Gadiformes	12	800	cod, hake
Lophiiformes	18	over 297	anglerfish
Atheriniformes	8	500	silversides
Cyprinodontiformes	8	807	killifish, pupfish, needlefish
Gasterosteiformes	11	36	sticklebacks, seahorses
Scorpaeniformes	35	1217	lionfish, scorpion fish, sculpins
Perciformes	148	9293	perches, mackerel, archer fish, barracudas, tunas, billfish
Tetraodontiformes	9	339	triggerfish, puffer fish, porcupine fish, ocean sunfish

Sharks

Sharks are cartilaginous fish. This chart shows the main shark orders.

Order	Number of Families	Number of Species	Examples
Dogfish sharks (Squaliformes) Short snout, mouth underneath, no anal fin.	7	94	dogfish, cookie-cutter sharks
Requiem sharks (Carcharhiniformes) Anal fin, 5 gill slits, 2 dorsal fins, no fin spines, mouth behind the eyes, nictitating (blinking) eyelids.	8	216	hammerhead sharks, tiger sharks, whitetip reef sharks, oceanic whitetip sharks, catsharks
Mackerel sharks (Lamniformes) Anal fin, 5 gill slits, 2 dorsal fins, no fin spines, mouth behind the eyes, no nictitating (blinking) eyelids.	8	16	great white sharks, thresher sharks, mako sharks
Carpet sharks (Orectolobiformes) Anal fin, 5 gill slits, 2 dorsal fins, no fin spines, mouth in front of the eyes.	8	31	wobbegong, nurse sharks, whale sharks

Where fish live

This diagram shows where some of the major fish species are found.

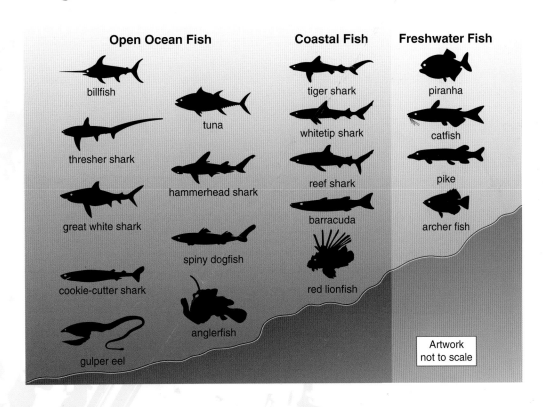

Open Ocean Fish
- billfish
- tuna
- thresher shark
- hammerhead shark
- great white shark
- spiny dogfish
- cookie-cutter shark
- anglerfish
- gulper eel

Coastal Fish
- tiger shark
- whitetip shark
- reef shark
- barracuda
- red lionfish

Freshwater Fish
- piranha
- catfish
- pike
- archer fish

Artwork not to scale

Glossary

adapted when organisms have special features that help them live in their habitat

algae small (often microscopic) plant-like organisms

barbels feelers

binocular vision seeing the same thing with both eyes rather than just one

brood young of an animal produced in one birth

buoyant/buoyancy able to float

camouflage colouring and markings that help a creature blend in with its background

cartilage tough, horny material that makes up the skeletons of sharks

corals colonies of tiny marine creatures that produce a hard chalky outer casing

coral reefs rocky underwater ridges formed by corals

digested when food is digested it is broken down into nutrients an animal can use

estuary wide mouth of a river

family group or genera of living things that are closely related

fertilize fertilization is when a male fish releases sperm, which then join with a female fish's eggs. The fertilized eggs can grow into young fish.

filter feeder animal that feeds by sieving tiny food particles out of the water

fins flaps sticking out from a fish's body that it uses to swim with

fry young fish

gestation period time from mating to birth

gills fish's 'lungs', in which it extracts oxygen from water

habitat place where an organism lives

hatchling fish newly hatched from the egg

larva (plural larvae) the young stage in the life cycle of an insect between hatching from an egg and adulthood

luminous something that shines with its own light

mangroves trees that grow in swampy conditions along the coasts in some tropical areas

mate/mating when a male inserts sperm into a female animal to fertilize her eggs

microbes microscopic creatures such as bacteria and algae

migrate to regularly travel long distances, either for food or to breed

organs structures within the body that have a particular job, such as the heart, lungs and gut

osprey bird of prey that catches and eats fish

parasitic living on or in another living creature and taking food from it, without giving any benefit in return

pelvic fins fins attached around the area of a fish's pelvis (hips)

plankton sea creatures that are too small to swim against the ocean currents and drift with the movements of the water

predator animal that hunts and eats other animals

pressure (in water) force pushing against or squeezing something in the water

prey animal that is hunted by a predator

pup young sharks

reproduce to give birth to young or to produce eggs that hatch into young

scavenge eat dead meat or rubbish

school (of fish) a large group of fish

sediment fine particles such as mud, silt or sand

sex organs body parts that males and females use to reproduce

silica glass-like material made from silicon

spawn fish eggs (noun) or when a female fish lays eggs in the water

species group of animals that are very similar and can breed together to produce young

sperm sex cells of a male animal

streamlined torpedo-shaped, so able to move through water easily

swim bladder air-filled space inside a fish that helps it to float in the water

womb place inside a female animal where her young grow and develop before they are born

yolk sac sac containing yolk – concentrated food for a newborn fish

Further information

Books

Sea Creatures: Sharks, Carol Baldwin (Heinemann Library, 2003)

Natural World: Encyclopaedia of Fishes, John R. Paxton, William N. Eschmeyer, David Kirshner (Illustrator) (Academic Press, 1998)

Encyclopaedia of Sharks, Steve Parker and Jane Parker (Firefly Books, 2002)

Sharks, Bernard Stonehouse (Facts on File, 1999)

The Shark Watcher's Handbook, Mark Carwardine and Ken Watterson (BBC Worldwide, 2002)

Life Series: Sharks, Michael Bright (Natural History Museum, 2002)

Websites

Zoom Sharks
www.enchantedlearning.com/subjects/sharks/
A website with lots of general information about sharks, and profiles of many individual species.

Nova Online: Island of the Sharks
www.pbs.org/wgbh/nova/sharks/
Video clips and interactive information about the shark-rich waters around the Cocos Islands in the Pacific Ocean.

Fishbase search
www.fishbase.org/search.cfm
Detailed information on a huge number of fish species.

Bony fish printouts
www.enchantedlearning.com/subjects/fish/printouts/bonyfish.shtml
Information on many bony fish (fish other than sharks), including piranhas, billfish and tuna.

Index